THE SOUTHERN GOSPEL DUET BOOK

24 Favorites

Arranged by

Tom Fettke

LILLENAS PUBLISHING COMPANY
Kansas City, MO 64141

CONTENTS

Jesus Is Lord of All

GLORIA and WILLIAM J. GAITHER

WILLIAM J. GAITHER
Arr. by Tom Fettke

For What Earthly Reason

D. R.

DOTTIE RAMBO
Arr. by Tom Fettke

CD: 1:07

19

Can He? Could He? Would He? Did He?

J. C. and D. L.

JOHN CHISUM and DWIGHT LILES
Arr. by Tom Fettke

*May be the same individual if you wish.

CODA

can, He could, He would, and He did._____

C7   F7   B♭

Can He? Could He? Would He? Yes, He

G7

can, He could, He would, and He did.

C7   F7   B♭   B♭13

We Shall See Jesus

D. W.

DIANE WILKINSON
Arr. by Tom Fettke

The King and I

M. L.

MOSIE LISTER
Arr. by Joseph Linn
Duet arr. by Tom Fettke

I've Been Through the Blood

J. T. and D. W.

JERRY THOMPSON and DARYL WILLIAMS
Arr. by Tom Fettke

42

My Faith Still Holds

W. J. G. and GLORIA GAITHER

WILLIAM J. GAITHER
Arr. by Mosie Lister
Duet arr. by Tom Fettke

*If tessitura is too low for upper voice

44

This World Is Not My Home

TRADITIONAL

TRADITIONAL
Arr. by Tom Fettke

What a Day That Will Be

J. H.

JIM HILL
Arr. by Tom Fettke and Randy Smith
Duet arr. by Tom Fettke

Restore My Soul

M. L.

MOSIE LISTER
Arr. by Mosie Lister
Duet arr. by Tom Fettke

He Will Pilot Me

CHARLES T. BAILEY

BYRON L. SMITH
Arr. by Joseph Linn
Duet arr. by Tom Fettke

CD: 1:41

Where No One Stands Alone

M. L.

MOSIE LISTER
Arr. by Joseph Linn
Duet arr. by Tom Fettke

Champion of Love

P. C. and C. C.

PHIL and CAROLYN CROSS
Arr. by Joseph Linn
Duet arr. by Tom Fettke

1. La - dies and gen-tle-men!__ May I have your at - ten - tion?

2. He left His home - town__ to en - ter this a - re - na, to

I want to in - tro-duce to you– In this cor - ner__ of the

raise His hands in vic - to - ry for me. An an - gry crowd cru - ci - fied__ this

82

'Til the Storm Passes By

M. L.

MOSIE LISTER
Arr. by Mosie Lister
Duet arr. by Tom Fettke

86

Stand Still and See His Glory

D. R.

DOTTIE RAMBO
Arr. by Tom Fettke

Take Off Those Rags, Lazarus

K. P. and B. C.

KIM PATTON and BILL CASWELL
Arr. by Tom Fettke

51
gain. Take off those rags, Laz-a-rus,
C D D
Take off those rags, Laz-a-rus!
55
Don't need those rags now,
G D D
CD: 2:14
Laz - a - rus; You're a - live, you're a - live, you're a - live.
G D/A A7 D
59 Stronger
Take off those rags, Laz-a-rus, Take off those rags,
E♭ E♭ A♭9
Stronger

All of Me
with
I Surrender All

Arr. by Tom Fettke

He Knows Just What I Need

M. L.

MOSIE LISTER
Arr. by Randy Smith and Tom Fettke
Duet arr. by Tom Fettke

I Will Glory in the Cross

D. R.

DOTTIE RAMBO
Arr. by Joseph Linn
Duet arr. by Tom Fettke

boast not of works nor tell of good deeds, For

Heavenly Love

V. B. E.

V. B. (Vep) ELLIS
Arr. by Josh McPheeters
Duet arr. by Tom Fettke

116

122

Let Me Touch Him

V. B. E.

V. B. (Vep) ELLIS
Arr. by Mosie Lister
Duet arr. by Tom Fettke

126

Do You Know My Jesus?

with

Jesus, the Son of God

Arr. by Joseph Linn
Duet arr. by Tom Fettke

Simply ♩ = ca. 80

*"Jesus, the Son of God" (G. T. Haywood)

Mel.

Oh, sweet won-der;

Oh, sweet won-der; Je-sus, the Son of God._____

130

132

My God Is Real

K. M.

KENNETH MORRIS
Arr. by Joseph Linn
Duet arr. by Tom Fettke

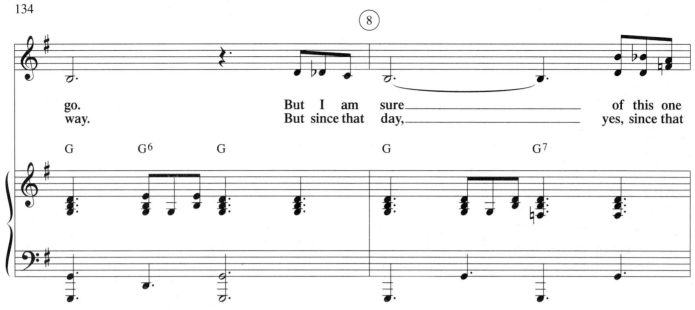

136

The Way of the Cross Led Me Home

M. L.

MOSIE LISTER
Arr. by Tom Fettke and Randy Smith
Duet arr. by Tom Fettke

138